The April Poems

The April Poems

LEON ROOKE

The Porcupine's Quill

Library and Archives Canada Cataloguing in Publication

Rooke, Leon
The April poems/Leon Rooke.

ISBN 978-0-88984-359-2

I. Title.

PS8585.064A67 2013 C811'.54 C2013-901066-1

1 2 3 • 15 14 13

Published by The Porcupine's Quill, 68 Main Street, PO Box 160, Erin, Ontario NOB 1TO. http://porcupinesquill.ca

Represented in Canada by Canadian Manda Group.
Trade orders are available from University of Toronto Press.

We acknowledge the support of the Ontario Arts Council and the Canada Council for the Arts for our publishing program. The financial support of the Government of Canada through the Canada Book Fund is also gratefully acknowledged.

Canada

Ontario
Ontario Media Development Corporation

Canada Council for the Arts Conseil des Arts du Canada

ONTARIO ARTS COUNCIL
CONSEIL DES ARTS DE L'ONTARIO

To ——

Carry us along, bright rider

Table of Contents

1. April's Father

Daughter, the law-and-order universe
has given way to chaos. Those blue skies
hold invisible thunder. Intelligent design
is the one true theory explaining the blackened meat
in your bowl of horrors. Be forgiving of your brothers
who knife Goth trade winds into your trim ankles.
Pay heed to your mother. Do not follow strange men
or scheming dogs into unknown abodes
however rank the appeal. Have it understood
that in this house we eat off the floor
as a lesson in fortitude. Which is why
we douse our lights the instant sun plummets.
Accustom yourself to incessant study
of suspicious school texts in the liquid gaze
of my wristwatch. That all is not roger
in this world should not steer you
into further indiscretion or onto the fields
of abstraction. Stay your focus and at bedtime
record a decent good night to all who love you,
not forgetting to remove your shoes.

2. April's Town

Now where to go to observe a bride's sweet breath
or the honey slang of citizens downing a fruity lunch.
In these parts we seek to convert to decency
the homosexual lampposts. I wanted someone to
kiss me and no one did. A stout man in a flamingo suit
asked me where I was going and I let him know
ignorance was mine. Sometimes the earth is no bigger
than the smallest town. This burg, for instance,
has but two people. I'm the other one.
We sleep on ice picks, I forget why.

3. April Defined

— What was it that attracted you to April?

— How I was made dizzy through love. How I came to see beauty in the strangest things. How modern art suddenly made sense. Her pluck, her prink, her plumelets. Her elegant feet.

— That's it?

— Clothes on the body, then the floor. I was eighty miles away and saw her naked in bed. She was saying smart things. I licked blue plates in cheap diners, thinking of her. Knowing that she was smarter than me. She was an intellectual colossus, big, big, and bigger. Call her up, you got busy signals, you got guys from Nantucket, Singapore, the Darwinian Isles. Because of her I could speak the language of wild dogs. Gypsies jumped from blackberry fields, shouting her name. Bees sacrificed their own air time to fly with her. Even wasps.

— What was it about you that made her keen?

— She liked digging me out of holes, where insects buried me. I introduced her to invisible birds which made nests out of her hat bands. I was a man of action who went out nights in a flying suit, in dyed underwear, stopping trains that otherwise would crash. I diverted streams so they'd trickle by our bedroom. I was savvy in the kitchen, slicing beets. I was a brave son of a bitch in the workplace, turning hot-headed thugs into limited-edition songbooks, Fords into schooners on Lake Huron. I enacted legislation making Mother's Day an extended foray through Greek isles.

— So you're saying your marriage worked out?

— Like the beauty of pure math. What did she say?

— Like juggling bricks in a hurricane.

4. April's Diary

We were made for each other, which means we suffered
four thousand heartbreaks weekly, these annually compounded.
He chopped vegetables and washed plates. I cooked.
Such activity identified the larger domestic roof
sometimes referred to as Our Continuing Development.
When we couldn't pay the rent we robbed banks.
We ate heart-bread, laced with hot peppers. We preferred
water-ground/stone-drained cornmeal, not that ashen stuff
        found up here.
But we did not obsess about Absolutes, even when Rehab
knocked down the door. Friends pitched rock-messages
through our windows: *Don't you two think it's time*
        you came out of there?
We want you for dinner next month (if the weather is nice).
We announced our run for Parliament seats
every third Wednesday (*if the weather was nice*). Otherwise,
we curled up on the floor with our dog: such a dear moment.

If I speak softly, he said, *may I hold your hand?* Well, goodness,
when was he not holding my hand? Once, we were profiled
in *Your Community Digest.* We loved reading about ourselves.
It says here, he said, *that in our youth we were wild subversives.*
I wouldn't have put it that way.... Subdued anarchists? I said.
We ever saw ourselves as A Developing Story.
We tuned in daily for updates.

5. April in Haiti

I was impressed
with the hat
on his lap
as we were instructed
in the ideals of marriage.
Divine was
a familiar word.
I was struck
by the polish
of the chosen one's shoes
and the white suit
we together picked out.
Everyone called him
by their preferred names:
Spider, Slim, Jocko, Firecracker,
Song Man.
We had to run to catch the bus
to Port-au-Prince.
Shots were heard.
He put a hand out the window.

    Bad (he said)
Worse coming.

I don't believe I replied. I think I never did.

6. April Lost

The Great Dark Faces
Storm from the bluffs
Surrounding us.

I surrender.

Don't shoot
Are the cries

One hears.

My own voice
Is an ache in the heart,
The soft mew of the cat
Before she falls dead.

7. April's 'Quoth the Raven'

Sam says to April, 'We've got to talk,'
but April has the music going.
He catches her later, drifting off to sleep,
he says, 'April, honey, we really must converse,'
April snatching a pillow over her head.
Come morning, Sam brings fruit and ginger tea,
flowers, newspapers, the mail, he says,
'Honey, the tension is building,
something's got to give, when
may we extrapolate?'

April gives Sam the level gaze (extrapolate?),
She's chewing that fruit, reading the news,
out spins a gay hand, April saying,
'Sam, I've told you a thousand times
I use up all my talk on women friends,
my throat needs a rest, all those chances
you had to talk but never did, I cannot possibly
believe you have one word to say of interest to me
in my lovely world, so will you kindly
shut up please?' — which is how all their talks end.

8. Not with That Attitude, Miss

April couldn't fly because Security refused to let her through. She had too many idiots in her suitcase. She explained to them that they were all former lovers, that she could not be held responsible for where they put themselves. Yeah, so you say, said Security, what's that you got in your shoes? Nothing, April said, once I remove my feet. Out of plain cussedness, they made April put her shoes on the belt. That suitcase stays here, they said. We are confiscating that trove of lovers. We are putting them in the same bag that holds ours. And, hey, do those triplet girls belong to you? April was having a fit. Why, she asked Security, are you making this so damned personal? The Security men she said this to told her she was their type woman. They'd looked all their lives for a woman who had her spit. You can't get on that plane, they said. You're coming home with us. We're mad for the mature damsel who travels with a shotgun under her dress. Ideal cleavage too.

9. April's Pets

When the canary chirped the children were sure it had eaten the cat. Fur was trapped in the beak. Something like a black tail was on the cage floor. April had to move their bed into a back room before the triplets were willing to try sleep. She had to read them pathetic stories about a gang of lizards making it big on Broadway. In the morning when the cat traipsed in they screamed. The cat was ghostly. It had ghostly eyes and in those eyes the children saw their future. The canary flipped. It didn't like the cat any more than they did. Well, that cat isn't Beethoven, April said. She opened a window and there went the bird, there went the cat. April dressed the three in bathing suits and took them to the beach. The whole beach crowd was walking on stilts into and out of the sea. The water was so calm you could write your name in the waves. You could set up housekeeping on the sea's floor. This is living, April said. Let's never go home. The girls agreed. Morocco next.

10. April's Continuation of the James Tate Poem 'Lewis and Clark Overheard in Conversation'

then we'll get us some wine and spare ribs
then we'll get us some wine and spare ribs
then we'll get us some wine and spare ribs
then we'll get us some wine and spare ribs
then we'll get us some wine and spare ribs

II. April's Note on Her Repeated Continuation of the James Tate Poems

One, I like Jim and like

his poems and

Two, because he lives

in Massachusetts

and can't hit me.

I am, however, as of this date

curtailing my drone strikes

on his property.

I am calling for negotiation

between principal parties.

12. April's Hundred-Yard Run

April ran a tulip posy into the end zone,
taking rank with the Packers man, Al Carmichael's
longest kickoff return, 106 yards in 1956. Good Friday,
I think it was, and predicted in the gospels.
That she did it pulling a wagon stacked
with broken furniture from St. Vincent de Paul
does not diminish the noble achievement,
given that 200 warriors from the Sioux nation
were dead-level intent on scoring her hide
with flaming arrows.
At the 50-yard line she paused to deliver
triplets seeded in god knows what awful place.
In the end zone, game-winning touchdown
against clicking seconds, she did the usual jig,
thumping her chest while executing cartwheels,
her tulip posy riding a wind into the uppermost
balconies where we sat groaning, saying to each other
what can you expect from a bunch of Indians.

13. April's Soul

'What's that?' the man asked, on a cold January night, having a smoke outside the No Frills Emergency Unit, April and the man shivering.

'This?' April said, and the man said, 'Yes, that,' and only then did April take a long look at the thing under discussion.

It was a thin, rather opaque thing, shoeless, standing about a foot high, wearing a plaid shirt, and also shivering.

'Maybe it wants a smoke,' the man said.

After a long time April said, 'No, that's soul,' and then they both studied the thing for a good many minutes, seeking some insight into its character. 'Well, why is it standing there staring at us?' the man said. 'What does it want? And as for that, whose soul is it? Is it yours or mine?'

'It's got blue eyes,' April at last said, 'so it must be mine.'

It was about this time that the man noted what a beautiful woman this woman was, and that she'd be quite a handful.

Both then saw a flash — let's call it a streaking light — and at that flash both April and the man made a startled jump, during which time soul shot back inside whichever one it had come from.

It was a short while after this that April and the man made a call to the Leave Right Now Travel Club.

Soul has proved pretty good company, liking a good laugh and partial to hot sand, lapping waves, a jazzy beauty in evening gowns. Tomorrow it is taking them on a picnic, followed by luxurious hedonistic nights at the Inn of the Blue Mountains Waterfall.

In the bars the man can sometimes be heard calling,
    'Two more quarts
For Delmore Schwartz!'

The triplets find all this tiring. They tend to sleep a lot.

14. April's Narrow Escape: The Early Years

Every time I get in the elevator to visit my boyfriend
these geese walk in and punch every button except mine
on the 64th floor. It doesn't matter which elevator
I enter or whether I race into another, there those geese are,
six of them, Ali Baba white, and they keep at it until I give up,
so it's been a week now I've not seen my boyfriend,
me and him calling back and forth, him saying I thought
you were coming and me saying what I say, him claiming
if I've got something on my mind then come out with it.
'Geese,' he says, 'you've got to be crazy or think I am,'
and such as that going off right and left.
I said to those geese tonight, Damn you, birds, quit
interfering with my life, a whole week now I've not
put my arms around him once, and the birds get all excited
the way they do, fluttering up and shrieking and pecking
holes in the walls, these feathers flying, and this one old
goateed goose honking, He's the wrong party for you, girl,
you ought to take a glance at his IQ, plus he's got
these other women riding these elevators night and day,
a goose down there with its beak around my leg,
everybody squawking, me shouting, Stop telling me these lies,
the elevator still at street level when this old grizzly
smelly drunk man staggers in, the geese falling silent,
deathly silent, till one flies up and whispers in my ear,
'That's the sorry old son of a bitch we're warning you against.'

Him?

Him?

'Yeah, him,' the bird says. And all is silent again while we whoosh to the 64th, I and the birds watching the old coot stumble down the hall, watching as he enters my boyfriend's very door, some woman shouting, 'Where the fuck you been?'

15. Found

Found on beach at Ravenel
one robust woman, 18 hands
high, raspberry-toed,
weight 14 flagonias,
chalk teeth, scar by left brow
(not recent), lips curled, singing
'Song of the Lost Archer' (b flat,
harmonizing w/sand/sea/salty air
marooned here score
the seasons (gauging by appetite)
belted grenades her simple apparel
long hair (blondish, a plum smell)
answering to the names Gertie
Myrtle, Judith, Edie, Eleanor
Veronika, Wong Su, Sweet Jesus
Darling, My Darling, Heavenly April,
restless of nights (though willing),
magna cum laude Seven Sisters college
if known
reply Box 1969
this paper,
soonest.

16. Found (Two)

Found on beach at Ravenel
by Tragalong Point
6 pm Fri. three dogs
in box labelled
DOGS — INDIA SEA CO.
Purebred blues, one m. 2 f.
vaccinations in good order
attentive, nourished, vigilant,
barks (throaty) twitchy (m.)
loving of sea, seabirds,
wind in trees
(lychee, longan, abiu, bilimba)
sway of rice in field, sway
of woman on Ravenel Beach
(see earlier entry) otherwise perky
if known
reply this paper,
now
skill-testing quiz req'd.

17. Island Woman

April scoops a paper washed up by the sea, each page intact, spreads these sheets above scrub bushes dressing the high dunes, peruses the pages as they dry —

> Descartes: 'I must insist, mon ami, ketchup on my French fries is a must.'

sets fire to those of low appeal (wars, plagues, politics —

> 'I am so tired of shooting civilians,' states a soldier of the Fourth Armoured Brigade) —

clothing ads, travel items, industry disclosures, comix, new gadgets for the kitchen, the pedantry of haywire right-wing columnists —

> 'bright new anti-pornography Kansas/Nebraska Dipstick Law: men to be hooded when checking vehicle oil; female/male elec. plugs shot down —'

Recipes extolling stuffed shish-ka-bob, stuffed asparagus stems, soups employing hearty beer. Such a bonfire April makes of this newsprint. Now shouting threats against the rising wind, the ocean's outlandish roar, she empties into her mouth golden ounces of McCallum's 18 purloined from crates rooted in sand, sets a fancy table for the evening meal —

grubs of the sea, rich harvest of lychee, longan,
abiu, bilimba, choochew nuts, one last coconut
split by thunderbolt only last week —

dines fastidiously, not omitting candles, the finger-rinsing bowl, thinking genetic responsibility, the laws of narrative disunity, thinking Beaumont & Fletcher's *'put 'er to the squeak and claw'd 'er bonnie weave'*, Decker's *'Climb again that tree and pluck that fruit which I aver I none ever tasted,'* thinking Genesis 2:24 *cleave (ye) unto (her) and be as one flesh*, thinking WHAT WAS I THINKING when I set sail to this place, bid adieu to Sam and my dear triplet daughters

sad is my cast
I in my suit
of disreptitude
whereupon
may I find
a word for
disreptitude
meaning of
adventuresome bent
of scholarly
if impulsive nature
perhaps it was
decrepitude
I meant
oh
where to find
a good district nurse

Rethinking with these thoughts highlights of her years to come with loving Sam, the very moment she will mount a life-sized painting of herself onto the ceiling over their king bed —

these dear love are my erogenous zones

At long last, with dreamy eye, looking out to sea, April moistens blackened stick to tongue, writes

Dear Paper:
I know this woman.
I do not recollect those dogs.

18. April and Henry James

And Henry James was weeping.
He was gushing tears,
Bright on his flushed cheeks as tiny marbles,
Having put to bed that minute
Tears of the Ambassador.
A young beautiful girl strode in
And said to Henry James
Seated in an English chair
By an English window:
Why are you crying?
Henry James said,
I am not crying, point of fact.
I am weeping.
April said, That is so cosmopolitan
It is almost divinity. But what
Is the diff?
Go away, said Henry James.
Return to Nebraska. Today
It is not my pleasure
To dispense sachets of sweetness
To American idiots.
April flung the English curtains
From the English window
As Henry James sat brooding.
My birth was in Manhattan,
Cautioned April, though I am now
Merrily Canadian. Or soon to be.

I have recently fled the arms
Of a famous, utterly experimental,
German novelist. I am
The baby in the family,
As was Gertrude Stein.
Dry your eyes, please.
I must see you clearly.
I like your new book's title.
I may enlist myself as your ambassador.
Henry James ceased his weeping.
I stand corrected, he said. Scant is the diff. Let's have tea.

19. April's Fashion Statement

We painted
the snowman black
that being the one paint can
we could open.
We painted
No. 2 fire station black
along with the stationmaster.
We painted the tulips black.
We painted a black man black
who hurled unlikely accusation
at our retreating numbers.
We painted
the paint can black
and blackened a shipment
of bananas from Ecuador
and the ship
and two other ships
containing unidentifiable objects.
Then we painted
the water black
and all the fish and baubles
haunting the water.
We painted
the sailors black
and all bemused citizens watching.
We painted mothers and fathers black
and their automobiles and abodes
and children
and all the dogs we could catch.

We were now entering our seventh day,
and April's street.

We liked April.

April's pretty feet
we only dipped in the bucket.

My toes, my toes! April said.

We were so fond of April's toes.
Those toes were our best citizens.

We said
April please
come home
with us,
we will cook up
a pot of black bean soup
and molasses cookies
and adore you forever.

April said,
Ask me tomorrow
when I am not so down in the dumps,
when I am not so much smoke up the chimney,
when my heart is not so much your blackened pavement.

This to us was reasonable.

Give us a kiss, then, we said,
and she did.

This was beautiful. This was so beautiful
it will live forever, a hardly there kiss
with wings into the future.

To finish up we painted
the daylight black
and when we were done
with the fine-edging
and every star unseeing
we painted each other black
and fell into our black beds
with our black hope
singing.

20. Utter Calm

I was out raking leaves when this flying woman dropped down
through swirly clouds. Forgive me, she said, you looked
so extraordinary down here among these amazing trees,
I've heard so much about.

I took her inside and made her a latte from the machine
brought back from Italy eons ago, delicate rewiring required.
Afterwards, the mister and I took her to Walmart for
a few special things. She said she hoped her debit card
would work. I was pleased it did. We invited her to dinner,
nothing elaborate, fresh corn on the grill or a stir-fry, perhaps
a glass of wine, but she said she had to 'get back'.
It seemed absurd to ask her where. We escorted her outside
and in a whir of utter calm she ascended into the heavens.

Naturally, the guy living next door poked out his head.
'I wish you happy bastards would move,' he said.
'We don't like that kind of business going on around here.'

21. April's Park Avenue Hats

For her lovers April
wore on the Wednesday
pink hat with red band

on Thursday
red hat
with pink band

Friday
yellow hat
with green band

some days   light green shirt
with   frolicsome collar
beneath   darker green tunic

some days   sheer sky-blue attire
    (those eyes!)
close to   nothing

sensible shoes always

and always lips unpainted
hair a golden trove
and always   the little trotting dog

each day these lovers saying
April   my god   April

A dollop of kindness please April!

April each day confessing
to her grandmother   Ida darling
I find   tomorrow
I must   dear heart
pawn
yet another of your
        Persian carpets
            Europe beckons
May we not come to terms
as concerns that addled dog?

22. Her Crossword Wars

A four-letter word beginning with F
Was the wife's request at the breakfast table,
So I put in a White House call
And instantly got the Commander-in-Chief.
What's cooking he says and I relate to him
the wife's present quandary. Are you one of mine,
he says, and I tell him damn so, through going on
eight alarming years. Excellent, he says,
and your wife is she also likewise one of mine?
So I shouted at her, Are you one of his,
To which she replies, No, mostly I am yours,
Although I do have my otherwise days.
Now here I feel I have to hedge the issue a bit,
knowing he's a sensitive joe, which is what
I'm doing when this underling intervenes,
that underling explaining to the pres
that it's something about a four-letter word
beginning with F, our leader next shouting,
Feet, feet, can't those sons of bitches ever
think for themselves?

23. Another Narrow Miss

We were driving along route 10, this man and me,
when we spotted a slew of men with guns,
some firing off into the woods, others with weapons
cradled like quiet babies, some down against the leg
like a walking stick. Turkey Shoot Today, 2 till 4,
my guy says, like he's taken up with a woman can't read.
He's stopped the car, he's saying, One thing I've never done
is shoot turkey on a Sunday afternoon when I'm out with
my best gal. This was in Louisiana where they find it
fashionable to talk like that. This man in coveralls
and wading boots, he drifts up, saying Good day
for a shoot, to me saying And the happiest of days
to you, M'am, what a friendly complexion you have,
reminds me of my sister over Choctaw way. Now, Mister,
will just you be shooting today or can I earmark my sheet
for you and the pretty missis both? My man
cocks an eye at me in a way that bespeaks
How did she get here, he and the turkey shoot master
next palavering in hushed tones about what I guess
will be the discounted rate, seeing as how
it is closing upon the closing hour, though I'm not
reckoning anyone will care if the shoot goes on
past sunset. Here my man comes with a low-budget
blue-barrel .22 air pump, the lady's firecracker for me,
a stockier item for him, looking like an old M1 carbine
to my eyes, 8-round clip, but what do I know?
Pull the trombone, says he, to reload, square off good,
squeeze the trigger, squeeze don't pull, eyes open don't flinch,
you think you got that? All along the road are strung
these men, kicking the dust, talking about shots
they've got off and what they've hit, or having a drink
of whatever has come in the thermos jugs. Now and then
a hunkering dog will poke its nose from the brush,
submit the patient stare before slithering back in.

My man is searching the trees and I hear him say,
'There's one dang my' — and I get a shot off
before he can say 'Hide', another saying
much the same, a full turkey volley lumbering up
on the far hill, me going at them slambang bang
bang bang … until the smoke is gone, the turkey sky clear.
At the room, come night, my man pokes at his beans,
says, 'Whatever's on your mind, kid, don't think
I'm hanging in with you,' wid-choo, adding
when I turn the level gaze on him,
'Some bitches who won't wear lipstick, refuse
a perm to the hair, know exactly how to spoil
a perfect day.'

24. Back to the Future: Is It All Folly?

dear you,

I've fallen into arrears

With all this

'love'
business.

I'll never

claw

my way free.

'must shrieks (sheets) reek
to invigorating pleasure? ...'

I am speaking to you, darling, from this dark chamber Miles.
Within. Earth.

25. Fragments Not from the Rose Room

(Sixth floor, Princess Margaret Hospital, October 4, 2008)

Did the trampled grass
Curse the stars
When last night
You left your sweetheart?

Something should be done
About the naked bride
Dancing in my soup.

The oak trees
On my street
Did not go bowling
Last night.
The elms sent out
For Chinese.

The ladybug
Was not amused
When told
Her outfit
Was anti-Christian.

Unpeeled mangoes
And green bananas
Lately have been seen
Driving Smartcars,
Always at incredible speed
And running red lights.

The wheelbarrow
Is desperate
To understand
Why so little
These days
Depends upon it.

My sweetheart's
Red shoes
Were no longer
Speaking
To each other.

One parting message
Was that a crocodile
Has never been admitted
To Bellevue
No matter
How desperate
Her situation.

The telephone
Is madly in love
With Martha and Dionne
(And George)
Seen last running
Goat Race goats
(Not that well)
In lovely Tobago.

Was the sun
Up to no good
When it ran off
With the postman?

Is the spring
Shower crying
Because
It has lost
Its darling?

The Syllabus of Love
Is missing page 2009.
Page 1969 is printed
Upside-down.
The index misspells
Most of our names.

26. Just to Be Clear About April's Politics

Bush in the war room
Generals gone
So quiet you'd think
Carpet layers
Had soundproofed
His thoughts
26 pens in pocket for signing a gratis bill
Water glass emptied
Under the table
Texas boots.
Don't shoot
He says to the opening door
In toes
The schoolteacher wife
  whispering
Honey, did you forget
Your way upstairs?

27. April and Harold

In her youth April, wanting happiness for everyone,
	promised a summertime lover
That if their lives didn't work out and love never came
	to much, or did and then
Went missing, they'd look each other up and perhaps
	snare the joy remaining for a
Pair who had called it quits.

Forty years passed and there was Mother saying,
	your old fling, Harold, asked about you.

April, desiring sun, relief from family woe, found herself
	saying to Harold, I'll pop in around three.

They met at Chicken Deelight, Harold managing the place,
	saying first, Is that you?
And next, I want you to know this is on me.

April had Tinkerbell's tea, chicken on a toasty bun,
	$5.49 it came to.

They caught up with each other in salient disregard of truth,
	Harold with his ex this
And his ex that, children in the world 'footloose'
	and 'fancy-free'.

He excused himself a time or two, to clear the counter,
    instruct a sweeper as to
The rubbish beneath his feet, April once to the washroom
    to moisten her neck
And contemplate a wealth of notices, No Service to Drunks,
    Booth Occupancy Twenty Minutes Max.

Parting, Harold said, That black Impala you see there
    is mine, April replying,
I travel on wind when wind avails me
Both saying   see you   take care now

April not taking too badly their empty hands waving.

28. April Down South

Monkeys gather on the road
Outside El Fundidor
Allowing no passageway.
At day's end they leap
Into each other's arms,
Happy Hour
Bananas and cake.

These monkeys
Have taken note
Of offence and defence
Common on sporting fields,
The pick and roll,
The four-corner trap
The top-hat steal
Backcheck/bodycheck,
The blitz, the dunk
To take you out.

Yesterday El Fundidor
Rolled in road sweepers,
Fork-lifters, 30-ton
Pavement Bulls

To no avail, monkeys
Jumping into cabs,
Stealing the wheel,
Driving these machines
Deep into forest
Midst a chatter so
Enthusiastic
You'd think they
Were children on a carousel.
At night they frolic,
They wed.
There will be more next year.

29. Like Tractors Clearing a Road

Her beloved reckoned April was a bit slow,
out there within the tornado's swoop
wearing a see-through dress, yellow hat, yellow boots,
collecting raindrops in big red buckets.

It won't work, he shouted,
mad as thunder to be loving a goddamn fool.

Days then afoot, cats prowling, ears high, pots boiling
In the yard where clothesline cloudline once hung
between now fallen trees, the sky icy blue,
she put polish to each raindrop,
strung them on glittering strings, tiaras,
and the like, pearl exquisiteness for 5th Ave. strutters,
nighthawk jubilants, Soho playgirls.

Ear studs, nose nuggets, lip, belly, toe,
And buttock necessities for
The mall bunch.

Make a killing in the Market,
Europe next.

A Once-in-a-Storybook thing, she said,
Now I'm on fire with passion
And want to go at love
Like we were tractors clearing a road.

30. April's Mattress Poems

The book picked up said *Poems*. I soon came to see this must be a prose book of poems. The headmaster smacked my head. To circumvent worse, I raised the issue with him. You must be a daft one, he said. Surely you must be. The real and the other thing isn't the issue. They are both frivolous pursuits only a sissy could love. If you were a real boy you would be down in the boiler room getting beat up by tough guys. I took off to the boiler room, where I learned all the tough guys had gone to see Little Brown Jug trot the half-mile at Yonkers. A girl in a slat chair by the furnace door told me that. As for prosy or the other she said Borges wasn't kidding when he said a man ought to roll up his cuffs when running in rain. 'But of course,' she said, 'people of his station would have neat socks.' It turned out this girl liked the sissy type. She plainly told me I could sleep in her bed, in another ten years. She had ten thousand poems, prosy and the other, sewn into her mattress.

There's a way of getting a poem to the page
without utilizing words.
It's like you call me to the phone
and all I hear is silence. What I am thinking
is, Whose silence is that? What message
is it imparting? Is this call for me
or for another party? Should I be fearful?
Will I survive the night?

'That's one of the poems,' she said. 'I like squalid poems.
I haven't sewn that one into
The mattress yet.'

31. My Personal Story

After my love was taken away I was without love and went one cold day to the Lovers' Lounge, a kind of Love Shelter in a part of the city I had never been before. Not much was going on, as far as I could see. A few bent people were huddled in the corners and the speaker-music, far from uplifting, exited to panic the broken heart. Strange to say, I returned during the coming weeks. Sometimes, if a tender was on hand, you could get a warmish drink at the bar. Come late night, the odd beggar couple might drift in a kind of death dance over the floor. Helium balloons, ribbons from the ceiling, inspired by god knows what saintly Committee of Volunteers, emitted a cheerless grace not dignifying the heart. The heart, in any case, was so thick with sorrow, you could eat from it with a spoon.

Night is the thin woman walking on stilts
the frozen sea.
She sleeps flannelled on your woodpile
through the vacant days.

You are a sailor swept away
without oars
to the paradisal cove
rarely seen.

Come brighter weather I sought again the Shelter housing the Lovers' Lounge. I found it boarded up, the roof collapsed, the entire neighbourhood blighted, distressed. A handwritten note taped to a broken window gave a number you could call should you have a valid beef. You might try the Museum of Civilization, no address given, rumoured to exist, if you still had the heart.

32. April's Great Google Deal

13 dollars the spacious Vegas suite
80% off dinner w/ complimentary champagne
free car, free driver, unlimited escorts
insurance we pay
deals at the wheel
free wake-up calls
free new shoes
free wedding dress
24-hour comp spa
comp salon (hair)
electrotherapy no charge
we will fly you anywhere
free free free
we love you so
we cry with the thrill
of so loving you

33. April's Bad Husband Day

Man came into April's kitchen
said he was deaf and blind
said he wasn't hardly human
said he loved no one
said kindness was a thing unheard of
said he couldn't hear his own voice
said divine providence had assured him
a cursed life
said Why are you looking at me that way
April and the children looking
chills raking the spine
knowing they knew him
from somewhere

34. April Dressed to Kill (Sam)

Hat from Panama
boots from Gibraltar
(spurs, Wyoming)
stockings from Brazil
dress the Americas
(Bergdorf Goodman
via Istanbul)
panties (pink blue
aspiration over each buttock)
belt from the Navajo Nation
(silver buckle bearing inscription
'Made by Pauper's Hand, Santa Fe')
dangly ear figurines decidedly Moroccan
chaps Francine of Bollywood
pearls (the Orient)
hair by Brubeckler
eyes by Miró
lips his brother
gloves (Duchamp, Calder)
perfume unknown though known
to be reliable
purse a Hell for Leather creation
of the Butterfield clan, New Plymouth
in April's purse (she's going incognito
today) a white pistol
(yellow barrel) two-shooter
a new salt shaker (Buddha model)
mints, comb, paper clips
lecture notes
pens and notebooks
tissue to catch the sobs
of a woman intent on murder

proper reading matter — Trollope,
Mansfield, Apuleius (A Metrical Version
of *Cupid and Psyche* and Mrs. Tighe,
G. Bell and Sons, London, 1911)
a letter from an admirer
(*you saved me, my thanks*, Royal Lodge
of the Upper Sorrow):
scissors, various knives, discreet poisons
a rope (silk) for strangling
Grimsby poppy seeds in
(pretty) Nantucket packet, fourteen
dollars (Canadian, Greek, Italian)
in coins.

Rogue. Rake. She would say.
          Then … bang
                    bang

                    drink this you brute.

Afterwards … I think (she would say)
an uplifting *aperitif*
at *chabbi chieu*
sanguine dispatch
of the killer instinct
never (rarely) acted upon
post-death theories rising
with every moon:

'Well mother, I loved
him enough to carry his best suit
through nettle fields. I sang him
melon songs in the nude. I danced
entire *weeks* to 'Wabash Cannonball'.
The suits in your field look better
than they do on him. A barber
never saw his hair. He neglected
the day I married him. May catfish
waddle his name.

So that, mother, is it for now
from me
here
smartly suited-up
in wifely
love.'

35. April's Fling

Mitsubishi, the man said. Mitsubishi. This was between acts, opening night of a miserable play. But the man kept saying Mitsubishi and peering into my ears. Each time he said it, he drew closer. Need I say I was advancing myself. I liked the look of him. I said, What's this Mitsubishi business? The man whispered Mitsubishi in my ear. He held my hand. He rubbed up against me. I did a bit of rubbing back. Mitsubishi, he said. I said, Hey, I know those wheels! Mitsubishi, he said. He had his arms around me. His lips were nibbling my neck. I felt all scrambled inside.

Oh, vice versa.

You betcha, vice versa.

People were looking at us. I guess they thought we were old friends. Some of those looking *were* old friends.

Mitsubishi, the man said.

We were rooting around in each other. My God, how we were rooting. You're the loveliest woman in the world, the man said. What a stroke of Mitsubishi we are both here. I looked around. There were about two hundred of us. Among the women, I was the tallest. No need to tell you, in my heels, I was the tallest. Mitsubishi, the man said. How tall you are! Tell me you love me, he said. He whispered this in my ear as we stood clutching each other. I wanted him to kiss my breasts. I wanted to pull up my top and tell him to do it. When I first had breasts, walking down the street, I wanted to raise my top to strangers and invite them to kiss my breasts. I really wanted that.

I wanted him to.

Mitsubishi, he said. Mitsubishi yourself, I said. If I did this, I said to the man, what would you do? I snatched up my top. I felt cool air on my breasts. My nipples were standing up like tree trunks. They were beaming like sunsets. I'd Mitsubishi them, he said. I'd Mitsubishi the dickens out of them.

Do it! I said.

He kissed first one breast and then the other. Then started over. His hands cuddled them. I wanted my whole body to leap into his mouth. Mitsubishi, I said. I was suddenly tearful, out of hearty trembling joy. Vice versa. Oh, vice versa.

My friends there had never looked happier. They were getting in a bit of Mitsubishi themselves. I could read their thoughts: April's out of the woods, they were thinking. Finally she is out of the woods.

We were definitely, for the minute, all of us out of the woods.

Lots and lots of vice versa.

Between acts.

Nibble-nibble, the man said. We've found each other. No more woods.

You betcha.

36. April: A True Love Melody

A terrible thing happened. This woman came rushing up to me and slapped my face. That'll teach you, she said. This is the terrible other thing she said. You're a heel, she said. Then she said yet another terrible thing. You're a louse. Don't tell me the word's out of fashion.

She'd run that far, all the way from how far she'd run, to say these terrible things.

I tried steering away, but she was steering too.

Because she was by no means done with the terrible things that needed saying.

You are such a little boy! she said. She was slapping and stomping. Saying these terrible things.

Such a baby! Did someone forget to burp you?

She had got her second wind.

Are you going home to Mama? she says. Is that where you're going?

Now she's leaving. She's said everything she wants to say.

And what I am saying is exactly nothing.

I am saying exactly nothing because with this woman there are times when you may not.

Did your mother forget to bronze your baby shoes?

She screams this out.

Grow up!

This, too, she screams out.

In a hurry now. Like now there is another emergency calling her away. Like there are another fifty people she's got to set straight.

A thousand fires she's got to put out.

Looking pretty darned adorable, actually.

I am thinking: Where was I going anyhow? What was my rush?

Wait! I shout. I'm coming with you.

Be quick about it, she says. I better get that ring tonight.

37. My Bride (Revisited)

My bride
comes with fruit
fruit trees, shrubs, herbs
an entire savannah strapped
to her back.

How softly the rain falls.

Look how slowly she advances along the road.
One more river to cross
and this young beauty
will be

an old woman

closing the door

on fifty years

of gruelling

            marriage.

38. What We May Learn from Dr. Phil About Becoming a Good Husband

Don't be the section-hand who goes through a spaying at shift's end and says I'm beat,
I'm the soup's ennui, I think I'll go home and sock a pillow.
Such is a famous unerotic turnoff
to the domestic enterprise,
to the many who are privy to wife and mother's
innermost cravings.

[pause for commercial]

Consider that your children have defected to a higher authority and regard you at home
dozing nightly in your chair like an exploded potato, no one yet giving the smallest thought
to the someone in the kitchen pretty soon having to make dinner.
Say instead something catchy,
something even a dulled party may clepe unto, words far afield from snipings on the order of
'My fetching beast, bring me a beer.'

[pause for commercial]

Like, be tender.

[violin in]

Like, where did you flop your boots?

[zinger]

Like, did you say Thank you?

[zinger]

Like, did you say Precious children, would you consider changing the channel to Dr. Phil?

[violin in — pause for commercial]

Don't come on as the tyrant who says I know who I am
but who you are
is a wiseass bottom-feeder.
This is really quite crass, unbecoming to the ideal husband and
contrary to universal standards
appropriate to our Homeland, whatever your race,
creed, whatever.
Be forthright as pertains
to problematic arenas, saying for instance, 'Honey, it has come
to my attention re sex
that immediate gratification of the solo partner leaves much
unresolved in the family dynamics.'

Say instead, 'Honey, where did you find those pretty shoes?'
another example of the tender. Or endeavour,
once upon your pillow, to casually remark,
'My dear, I am bewitched
as never before by your incredibly attractive cheekbones.'

[pause for commercial
station ID
community-service spot]

Do this and your erotic powers will increase tenfold,
as has been foreshadowed in divine text,
although this does not mean your full body of crimes
will be forgiven or bring
slack to the tight fists of your grim children.

[full-screen graphic]

A final point, my brethren, is thus and so:
the favourable family hour
should make allowances for the unbelievable, the unavoidable,
the not quite acceptable. Do not on any occasion
bolt your feet to the floor
when kissing the mother of your children. Follow these edicts
and you will have wrung tranquility out of chaos, at least until
my next show.

[promotion — 'Tomorrow Dr. Phil will …']

39. April's (Bobby Darin) Song

oh give me back our game
the who was the what was the whence you came

give it to me good and true
return to me the other you

doowat dee doo ooo

to Perchance let us flee
such a happiness it is I see

give unto me the other you

doowat dee doo ooo

before I'm dust
before I'm through
the you that is me
the me that is you

love making love making two

return to me the self
that is you

doowat dee doo ooo
doowat dee doo doo doo

40. Lunch with April

Did you hear what I said?
What?
That she'd like to shoot you and send you home in a crate.
She never liked me.
Does anyone?
That's alarming. Have we not always been best friends?
You're like Canada. Too much ice.
I love that woman. I can't help myself.
Send flowers. Don't forget her birthday.
Okay.
You forgot mine.
I was in the Yukon up to my eyeballs.
With some wench, I expect.
Do you have spies?
Not that many. They've mostly retired.
I'm the retiring type myself.
Your worthless life has been well-documented.
    Shall we order lunch?
Let's wait. You know she's always late.
I'm kissing her first.
Okay.
She'll likely arrive with her usual gay entourage.
Or on her trike churning those wheels.
Pursued by admirers trotting fast.
She claims a single veering off-course.
    She claims her hands were tied.
She thinks she owns this town.
She owns me though I never received one cent.
She got us both cheap.
I was always cheap. It was from my reading classics as a lad
and running around with witless sheep.
Such does give one the moral edge.
I'd like to bite her neck.

That would have consequences too frightening to conjure.
She digs me. She said I'm hot.
You're not hot. Meat on the spit.
I'm fit.
You're a mommy's boy.
The ship ahoy.
Let's forget April. Speak of something else.
There is no Else.

41. April Makes Her Stand

You have never loved me.
You're hooked on (dare I say straddling)
that lilac woman in the Chekhov story.
Never seen (the faceless slut)
but always that hint (how I
despair of you) in every room.

Now as for wealth
I contend I am among the top
two percent of wage-mavens
in the whole of North America.

If I am proved right,
then I demand your undying love
and sex on demand, ignoring
for the moment my liege of trifles.
('Lower the shade, Iona,
that man across the street
is looking at you!')

If, however, I am proved wrong,
I will consent to the release
of all pleasures, and race
like a bent chicken
into every room,
with (Cr)(h)appy Lilac Spray.

42. April's 'No Frills' Poem

wellwell the well is dry
the grey goose is gone
welwelthwel i dr
thgregoos i gon
wewe t we d
t gr goo go
www
g go g

-   -   -

-

-       -

43. April and the Bad Bees

A woman in the laundromat said to April, The bees are truly nasty this year. April was quite at a loss in what manner to reply, then noticing the speaker was addressing another woman to her rear, though only because this other woman replied to the first, Yes, I have never seen them so bad as this year. I do not believe these are our standard-type bees. No, these are mating bees, said the first, both women then settling heavy glances on April and her triplet daughters occupying a three-seater pram. April inserted another quarter in the dryer. The women sat in green plastic chairs, talking away about the nasty copulating practice of these repugnant bees, being quite explicit, even vulgar, even pornographic, was April's thought, not liking either the glances coming her way, as though she personally was to blame. They swarm a person, this one woman said, they hold her down until all have had a go at her, and then they swarm away and do the same to someone else and no one says a word. Yes, the other said, it is even worse at my house. They tie us to the beds, they sup on our toes, they regard us as slaves, even the mites have noticed. Whereupon the women fell silent for some few moments, content to watch the clothes swirling in the dryers. April's triplets whimpered. Then the one woman said, What I think is that this queen bee business is a lot of rubbish. No queen in her right mind would permit such appalling behaviour. You think it is a king, then? asked the second. Why, of course, came the rejoinder, some nasty despot king, have you not known them by the thousands? The two women at this point rutting a final malevolent glance upon April, then lifting their wings and flying off into abysmal night.

44. April's Clunker Car

conked out on a high rise
not that far from Indian Country,
where she knew people. A tow-truck guy,
there in an instant, said he'd noticed her condition
round about the Tonawanda River
up by Singalong, the best part of three days ago.
April in the cab beside him, he confessed
he'd been on her tail pretty much the whole of her life.
I ought to have married you and not that other party,
he said, not to claim I could have done any better
at the time and not that there'd been any chance
of getting out of the thing
without losing my kids.
They are doing okay, he said,
about the same as yours.
Nice to see you holding up so well.
Yup, well, here you go, he said,
pulling into a hustling hub,
next time you're in trouble
breathe deeply and I'll be on your bumper
like a hurricane.

45. On the Ropes

Love needs new shoes
but is out of work.
Last night love was arrested,
Drunk, Your Honour,
leaning against a lamppost.
Did she resist your advances?
Yes, she did, now you mention it,
plus she spat on my boots,
vile language, too.
Take her to an alley, the judge said,
beat her to a pulp.

Love staggered away blind
hot wires barbed in her breast
some bones broken
and now naked of foot
in fact naked head to toe
bleeding rather a lot.
Not that anyone much looked:
pretty autumnal day
old bruised ugly broad
bent like that.

46. April Contemplates God

1) God Wakes Today

God wakes today
Without a thought on his mind.
It's as if he's been put out to graze in an idiot's head,
If that idiot is an idiot unable to find the shower stall,
Refuses to shave, or found himself out here
In cloudland up to his jockstrap, up to his eyeballs,
Aimlessly floundering. Is it the seventh day
All over again? And who is that lean, bearded guy
Over there bleeding on my Cadillac? Ow, yow,
Was there revolution while I slept? O good,
Here comes a fleet of angels, such lovely feet,
Will they — (what's the word?) — k-k-k kiss me?

2) God's Snit

Sausage sizzled in a pan, Wonder Bread branded with his name
GOD, by Luke's hot poker, scallion stirred up in the grits,
About a gallon of water to kill this hangover, well, that might suffice
For breakfast. Then some high-profile Christian army
To defang Luke the Creep and all those other has-beens
Defiling my doorsteps. Get that g-d dollhouse off my balcony,
promote a few wars, paint my toenails, study tomorrow's blueprint,
and that will do it for this hour, think I, I, I Think, Think, Think
(Would you kindly shut your trap while I am) Think Think Thinking
You can go to blazes if you imagine I, I, I am giving note
To those whispers in my trees or making any
house calls this dumb day.

3) God's Haircut

That clown, Luke, hidden partners the other three, has opened a new barbershop in what he calls The Golden Realm, up here in the Early Restoration area where mostly ancient saints persevere. There flits one now, hand in hand with his child bride. God is Luke's first customer, no charge, in for a shave and trim, few highlights, faint tucks in the chin, wavy sweep over the brow akin to that Trump guy. Celebrity trackers are on hand, as you might predict, this kingdom aflow with unknowns, the nobodies, those rowdies whose first birth didn't take, the poor, the poor, God is so fed up with those knee-bent jugglers ever crying like stricken hyenas. Get a life, he'd be telling them. Had he not forsaken pulpits after boomerang thunderbolts practically beheaded him. Not to mention those wild Indians on his tail. Today a band plays, out of tune as bees on a merry-go-round, for when did these tubby tuba-goons care to learn proper music? Well, yes, opines Luke, they do lack Elvis and Lady Gaga's (sainthood now) after-burn, it's hardly the same as when the Royal Wedding's Steeple Choir broke a gut on your Messiah Jig and fifty thousand geese altered course. Tuba thumpers come cheap, Matthew, Mark and John pithily confirm. God, under the lather, worries that no one is saving his sacred locks covering the floor, all has gone downhill fast, squatters galore, this autarchy hardly the jewel envisioned in fabled script. A minute ago he was sure he spotted his 'only begotten's' mum out there among the multitude. He's heard that cunt lately has been hitting the tables, dropping princely sums, stirring up her own Virgin's Homebrew. No one ages here but somehow she whacked out, turned senile, canoodles strangers, doesn't answer to her own name, cavorts with that Mohammed bunch, lifts gangrened eye to the trillion candles honouring the historical deed. Okay, she was duped, but what can you say to a sweet peasant girl brainless as a tick?

Luke's done. He's shaking on the powder, removing the smock. The partners take to the street with collection plates. Nothing is free here, inspiration being a costly affair. How to keep the rabble out? God sees security walls stretching a thousand meters above the clouds, those clouds seeded with toxic rain ('no more namby-pamby crap'), stamp out the lice, the dirty feet, the noisome harangues. Curfews next, the neat police state. Talk to my 'only behoven' son. We are the best they have, so long our long light over the seas. El Supremo, I mean. When were the days I couldn't rise from my bed, poisons funnelled into my ear, and I had to pray to myself, such an embarrassment that was. Wheel me to yon balcony, brother Luke. Ermine me. I want to arouse the troops with a few impromptu words: *Am I not you? Am I not as one with your vicissitudes?*

4) God Is Not In Today

I was down this path before and know its end.
No Where. No Where is a No Place
I've known in the long ago as in the nights before
When they shackled your ankles
And would have done the same to sun and moon
Had they not hidden.
Which they did for so long stars became morose,
Begging for the old company.
Their pleas went unheeded in the Great Darkness,
Which was a darkness leading
To this path. Blind path-builders brazenly logging
The virginal forest.
There are a thousand such paths, each in the end
Dwindling into this No Place,
This No Where. One day there will be dwellings here,
Perhaps a city. We will call it
Wasteland, the Wastelands, Land's End, or allow
It to be chronicled
By its patented name, Heaven.

47. Come On, Lamented April: Be Happy

So much was done to make us laugh, including the earth's flip-side up (it wasn't that pretty) and the moon's far side down (had its charm). Billie Bob did a song that was laughable, but didn't bring a smile. The Metric choir came on as men, which was not remotely cheering. Three (farm) roosters cakewalked (not funny), the Johansons pantomimed a recent fishing trip (horrendous), a sailor boy kissed my sweetheart's neck (grotesque liberty). Ms. Sullivan of the Labrador clan demonstrated her skateboard wizardry (one leg, two hands). Two Ottawa sisters recited poetry (deadly) through tin cans. There were the usual lectures (noble effort) in unknown tongues while some of us frequented the firing range (no hits). Everyone told jokes, mostly of our leaders leaping from flaming aircraft (these had possibilities). A report was given on our stockpiled smallpox virus and Israel's professed entertainment of compromise offers. (Ha-ha, someone said.) The Radiance came and went, no news there. It was only when walking home that we laughed. A deep trench opened up in front of us, removing our entire congregation head-to-hell into a riotous world where only happiness was allowed. Credit April for this.

48. April's Deep Remorse

has as cause three grown-up daughters
who last night received a lifetime ban
from the Epicure on Queen Street.
They claim innocence: *We were meek ravens*
with barely a chirp. It was that theatre bunch
settling old scores, flit and flame
and hands up the dress. Troubled Gertrude,
hemlock ear, Cassandra's bitter tongue:
Your mistresses do nothing but eat ice cream
all day! You would not cross the room
to spit if my very heart was on fire!
Your Master splits His own tongue!
His flaws are greater than the sum of yours!
Seven police cars racked the chains on twelve.
Lady, didn't I just arrest you? The Epicure
is the latest haunt hobbling April's troupe.
Not even the Brunswick House
will have them. *We can't go anywhere.*
Devout Muslim, Divine Bastards,
kicked us out. Ratsuck Tim Hortons too.

49. April Affirms She Married Well

I was his pearl of a girl
his twenty-piece orchestra
with perfect legs
his long hedge with naughty blooms
lithesome gypsy curse
spritely gin fizz
his bright sun
bursting
every pane

50. Thou Beside Me Singing

April's friend Tate wanted to know where went the lofty rhymes, the shimmering radiance in a poem's long ago. He liked those words cadenced light as a bird, say one of those that can hold still against raging wind, stop and start words from an eloquent brain, a hummingbird, April thought he meant. Fancy syllables espaliered onto a page like a peach tree clutching a drain? Yeah, something like that, Tate said, but making sense, you know, ordinary sense, like I don't have to get out my Ph.D. Pretty words, like you're the critic, where did they go?

+

April always wrote in a good clear hand:
Grass is first to hold the snow.
Blue lilac on my window did grow.
The girls drove me crazy today,
So did so and so.

+

April said to Tate, I keep my best words in a drawstring bag around my neck.

+

Those were the days.
She didn't say when.

+

She was ever at us, this intelligent woman poking the hornets' nest.

+

Don't wake the triplets. They'll never get back to sleep.
Those girls sleep too much.
If you had to chase them you wouldn't think so.
I wore myself out chasing you.
Liar, liar, what's on fire.

+

Dear Tate: It is a lie that beautiful words have disappeared. I have myself a trunkful in the attic, and thousands more buried underground. April has a stash in small jars in the pantry, falsely labelled *Spices.* The girls hide theirs in nine teacups in the three dollhouses, No Admittance to Anyone. Many fine words, luminous phrases, died on the battlefield. Pirates stole many. Coiled serpents, oiled evangelists. The Pentagon has ten thousand, no food, no water, locked up in distant prisons. In some cities ebullient words thrive — Moose Jaw, Sioux City — living on chocolate eclairs, butternut bread, turnips. They are home before dark. They dislike fanfare.

About the Author

An energetic and prolific storyteller, Leon Rooke is a writer whose work is characterized by inventive language, experimental form and an extreme range of characters blessed with distinctive voices. He has written a number of plays for radio and stage and produced numerous collections of short stories. It is his novels, however, that have received the most critical acclaim. *Fat Woman* (1980) was shortlisted for the Governor General's Literary Award and won the Paperback Novel of the Year Award. *Shakespeare's Dog* won the Governor General's award in 1983. As a play, *Shakespeare's Dog* has travelled as far afield as Barcelona and Edinburgh. *A Good Baby* was made into a feature film. Rooke founded the Eden Mills Writers' Festival in 1989. In 2007 he was invested into the Order of Canada. Other awards include the Canada/Australia prize, the W.O. Mitchell Literary Prize, a CBC Fiction Prize, the North Carolina Award for Literature and two ReLits (for short fiction and poetry). In 2012 he was the winner of the Gloria Vanderbilt Carter V. Cooper Fiction Award. Recently, Rooke's novels *The Fall of Gravity* and *Shakespeare's Dog* were produced in translation in new editions for distribution in France and Italy, two countries where his work has been received with great enthusiasm.